M000074147

I'M PREGNANT. NOW WHAT?

A PORTABLE GUIDE TO A
HEALTHY, HAPPY PREGNANCY

PETER PAUPER PRESS, INC.
WHITE PLAINS, NEW YORK

Our Company

In 1928, at the age of twenty-two, Peter Beilenson began printing books on a small press in the basement of his parents' home in Larchmont, New York. Peter—and later, his wife, Edna—sought to create fine books that sold at "prices even a pauper could afford."

Today, still family owned and operated, Peter Pauper Press continues to honor our founders' legacy—and our customers' expectations—of beauty, quality, and value.

With special thanks to Jessica Cohn, Barbara Paulding, and Paula Spencer Scott, who contributed to this guide.

Illustrations copyright © Olga Zakharova, used under license from Shutterstock.com

Designed by Margaret Rubiano

The publisher has made every effort to ensure the accuracy of the information in this pregnancy guide. Nonetheless, medical information changes frequently, and we advise the reader to consult a physician in matters relating to health. Peter Pauper Press cannot be held liable for any errors, omissions, or inconsistencies.

TABLE OF CONTENTS

INTRODUCTION

CONGRATULATIONS!

The journey from newly pregnant woman to full-fledged mother is filled with so much, it's helpful to have a special place, like this, to record your milestones and keep track of all the essentials. Ahead are great highs (like the first time you feel your baby move within you) as well as a few lows (like nausea or a backache), and lots of wonders and surprises in between.

Use this handy take-along tracker as a place to record all the details of appointments and tests. Fill-in charts help you compare and choose health practitioners and childbirth classes, and track fetal movement and contractions. Checklists of baby equipment and labor bag essentials help you remember what you'll need. And then there are places to keep notes and thoughts on your incredible journey to motherhood!

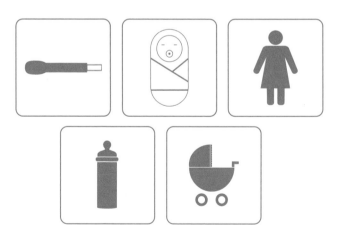

STARTING OFF

Welcome to the brave new world of pregnancy! You're beginning an amazing, thrilling, and topsy-turvy season of your life, from the first days through week 40. Here's wishing you a happy and healthy pregnancy, and smooth sailing along the way.

FIRSTS

The day I found out I was pregnant, and what that was like

Who I first told the news to

When I first felt pregnant

First doctor visit

First heard the baby's heartbeat

Day I first wore maternity clothes

Day I first felt the baby move, and what that was like

Other firsts

IMPORTANT CONTACTS

In the busy, exciting months to come, it's handy to have your essential contact information in one place.

Hospital or Birth Center ....

Contact information ....

Obstetrician ....

Contact information ....

Midwife ....

Contact information ....

Health insurance or cost provider ....

Contact information ....

Details ....

Pharmacy ....

Contact information ....

Labor Partner ....

Contact information ....

Pediatrician ....

Contact information ....

Other Contact ....

Contact information ....

CHOOSING THE DOCTOR OR MIDWIFE

When picking a doctor or midwife, here are the questions to find out what you need to know. Keep your practitioner referrals and notes about the interviews all in one place.

	PROVIDER 1
NAME OF DOCTOR OR MIDWIFE	
Contact information	
Date and time of interview	
What are the office hours, length of visits, and average wait?	
Details of costs and coverage	
Where do you deliver babies? Is an anesthesiologist there in case of emergency cesarean?	
Percentage of patients for whom you deliver babies yourself?	
Who sees me when you are not available?	
What tests do you do and when?	
Training, professional credentials, and length of practice?	
How do you handle slow labor? Pain management?	
Which medical procedures might you perform (episiotomy, fetal monitoring, IV) and when are they optional?	
What percentage of patients has had epidurals? Episiotomies? Assisted deliveries? Cesareans?	
Do labor, delivery, and recovery occur in one room?	
Can the baby room in? Is there a nursery? Someone to assist with breast-feeding?	
Notes (friendliness of staff, comfort in conversations)	

Note: The office staff may be able to answer many of the questions by phone.

PROVIDER 2	PROVIDER 3

MEDICAL HISTORY

Be ready with written information, rather than relying on memory.

YOUR MEDICAL HISTORY

Birth date ....

Date of last menstrual period .... Weight then ....

Contraception ....

Fertility treatments, if they apply...

Frequency & duration of periods .... Between-period bleeding ....

Age when periods began ....

Specifics

Medications (including over-the-counter medicines, vitamins, supplements)

....

....

....

Blood type ....

Allergies ....

....

....

Immunization record (include dates)

    Measles ....

    Mumps ....

    Rubella ....

    Chicken pox ....

    Tetanus ....

    Flu shots ....

Illnesses requiring hospitalization (include dates) ....

....

....

....

Injuries requiring doctor's care (include dates) ....

....

....

....

Surgeries (include dates) ....

....

....

Other pregnancies

Number of pregnancies, including this one and any miscarriages or terminations? ....

CHILD'S NAME	BIRTH DATE & WEIGHT	# OF WEEKS	HOURS OF LABOR	EPIDURAL OR OTHER MEDS	VAGINAL OR C-SECTION

Complications:

Bleeding after week 12 ....

Depression exceeding 2 weeks ....

Early labor ....

Ectopic pregnancy ....

Gestational diabetes ....

Miscarriage/termination ....

Placental problems ....

Toxemia ....

Other ....

LIFESTYLE	YOU	YOUR PARTNER
Smoking		
Alcohol		
Recreational drugs		
Prescription drugs		
Calcium supplements		
Caffeine use		
Exercise		
General nutrition		
Chemical exposure		
Radiation exposure		
Other		

Note lifestyle adaptations and concerns here.

YOUR FAMILIES' MEDICAL HISTORIES

GENETIC CONDITIONS	YOU OR YOUR FAMILY	YOUR PARTNER OR HIS FAMILY
Chromosomal abnormality		
Cystic fibrosis		
Down syndrome		
Hemophilia		
Huntington's disease		
Multiple births		
Muscular dystrophy		
Neural tube defects: Anencephaly, Meningocele, Spina bifida		
Neurological disorders		
Phenylketonuria		
Sickle cell anemia		
Tay-Sachs		
Thalassemia		
Other		

MEDICAL CONDITIONS	YOU OR YOUR FAMILY	YOUR PARTNER OR HIS FAMILY
Anemia		
Allergies		
Arthritis		
Asthma		
Autoimmune disorders: Lupus, rheumatoid arthritis, other		
Cancer		
Diabetes		
Heart problems		
Hepatitis		
High blood pressure		
High cholesterol		
Kidney disease		
Mental illness		
Thyroid problem		
Other		

COMPLICATIONS WITH PREGNANCIES	MOTHER	SISTERS
Bleeding after week 12		
Depression exceeding 2 weeks		
Early labor		
Ectopic pregnancy		
Gestational diabetes		
Miscarriage		

FIRST TRIMESTER

All of pregnancy is a transition—but the first trimester feels especially so. These first weeks are all about getting used to the idea of being pregnant and doing what you can to safeguard the well-being of the new life you're carrying. Do what's in your power to give your baby a great head start by shoring up your health habits. Ideally, you would have a preconception exam, before pregnancy begins. But don't worry if you've conceived before such a medical exam. There's still plenty of time to begin great prenatal care and to take care of yourself and your baby.

FIRST TRIMESTER CHECKLIST

- ✓ Determine date of last menstrual period. *Jan 27, 2020*
- ✓ Estimate due date. *Nov. 2, 2020*
- ✓ Begin a nutrition program. *sure*
- ☐ Determine details of medical costs and coverage.
- ☐ Determine your budget.
- ☐ Determine details of employer's family leave policy. *we have a meeting scheduled*
- ✓ Get recommendations for ob-gyns or midwives.
- ✓ Choose the doctor or midwife or both. (See pages 8–9.)
- ✓ Put together your medical history. (See pages 10–15.)
- ✓ Begin and track your prenatal checkups. (See pages 20–23.)
- ✓ Start prenatal vitamins.
- ☐ Begin medically-approved exercise program. *I got one... just haven't started yet*
- ✓ Make sleep a priority.
- ☐ See the dentist. *Sorry, can't, coronavirus*
- ☐ Look for versatile maternity clothing. *or wear sweats all day because you work from home now*
- ☐ Update your will or living trust. *Don't have one (yet)*
- ☐ Update life insurance. *Don't have it (yet)*
- ☐ Take photos and collect keepsakes. *?*

CHECKING IN

Here's the place to take note of your feelings, observations, and milestones during the first trimester. Use this page also to take note of things to remember or to follow up. Or just doodle—relaxation is good for you.

FIRST TRIMESTER DOS AND DON'TS

DO . . .

- ✓ Make an appointment with an ob-gyn, midwife, or family doctor as soon as a home pregnancy test confirms the news.
- ✓ Take your prescribed prenatal vitamins daily, if you can.
- ✓ Start making shifts toward a healthier, well balanced diet as soon as know you are pregnant, if you haven't already.
- ✓ Target nutrients you especially need now. They include:
  - *Iron.* Necessary for hemoglobin in the blood. Found in dried fruits, grains, legumes, and dark, leafy vegetables.
  - *Folate.* Helps prevent neural tube defects. Your prenatal vitamin contains it, but it's also found in breads, cereal, and pasta (fortified), as well as legumes, soy, brewer's yeast, and dark leafy veggies.
  - *Calcium.* Builds fetal teeth and bones without depleting your reserves. Low-fat yogurt or milk, dark leafy greens, and salmon are sources.
  - *Zinc.* Helps fetal growth. Found in fish, eggs, milk, and wheat germ.
- ✓ Keep moving. Run your current exercise routine by your health practitioner. The benefits of exercise to mood, baby, energy level, and overall well-being are tremendous!
- Schedule X-rays after the first trimester, if possible.
- ✓ Stay away from insecticides and fungicides, harsh chemicals, aerosols, and lead (in some paints and pipes). Other potentially dangerous substances include rubber cement, stains, finishes, and varnish and paint removers.
- ✓ Enjoy couple time.
- ✓ Dream a little. Don't get so caught up in the medical advice and planning that you neglect to begin to imagine your future baby, your new family.

DON'T . . .

- ✓ Smoke or spend time around people who do.
- ✓ Drink alcohol.
- ✓ Use other known damaging substances. These include: marijuana and other illegal drugs; tanning booths; douches.
- ✓ Heat it up. Skip hot tubs, whirlpools, or Jacuzzis during pregnancy, as it's not a good idea to become overheated.
- ✓ Handle or eat raw meat, raw seafood, or raw eggs, to avoid bacteria and parasites. Also skip rare hamburgers or steaks, unpasteurized milk or juice; and Caesar salad dressing.
- ✓ Change cat litter. Recruit someone else to do the job, since handling cat feces raises your risk of contracting the parasite that causes the infection toxoplasmosis. Also wash your hands after handling a cat, and keep cats off tables and countertops.
- ✓ Be blithe about vitamins, supplements, and herbals. Once you know you're pregnant, even before your first prenatal exam, call your doctor to run through any prescriptions or supplements you now take.
- ✓ "Eat for two." Your caloric needs barely rise in the first trimester—about the equivalent of an extra glass of milk. Most women need to gain only 3 to 4 pounds in the first trimester.
- Go overboard on the baby gear. Give yourself this trimester to get a firm grounding on what's happening in your life first.
- Obsess too much. Women have been having babies forever. Remember that being relaxed is more useful to your well-being than over-worry.

FIRST TRIMESTER CHECKUPS

Commit your first prenatal checkups to history and keep track of your questions. During the first trimester you'll be visiting your practitioner at least once every four weeks. Take note of details. Keep your questions and concerns, and the responses to them, handy.

Date/time .... Practitioner ....

Weight......................... Blood pressure .... Pulse ....

Fundus height .... Fetal heart rate ....

My questions & concerns ....

....

....

Responses & instructions ....

....

....

TESTS DONE OR ORDERED ....

....

Details and results ....

....

Follow up ....

Date/time .... Practitioner ....

Weight .... Blood pressure .... Pulse ....

Fundus height .... Fetal heart rate ....

My questions & concerns ....

....

....

Responses & instructions ....

....

....

TESTS DONE OR ORDERED ....

....

Details and results ....

....

Follow up ....

....

Notes ....

....

....

....

Date/time .... Practitioner ....

Weight .... Blood pressure ....Pulse ....

Fundus height .... Fetal heart rate ....

My questions & concerns ....

....

....

Responses & instructions ....

....

....

TESTS DONE OR ORDERED ....

....

Details and results ....

....

Follow up ....

Notes ....

....

....

....

Date/time .... Practitioner ....

Weight .... Blood pressure .... Pulse ....

Fundus height .... Fetal heart rate ....

My questions & concerns ....

....

....

Responses & instructions ....

....

....

TESTS DONE OR ORDERED ....

....

Details and results ....

....

Follow up ....

Notes ....

....

....

....

SECOND TRIMESTER

For most women, the middle of pregnancy is a relatively calm period. Energy tends to pick up; nausea subsides. Your bump becomes noticeable. And many women enjoy a new voluptuousness, more lush hair, and brighter skin, too. Not that it's all smooth sailing. It's also perfectly normal to continue to feel ambivalent or apprehensive about what's happening.

You may find that your thoughts start shifting from what's-happening-in-my-body to *who's*-that-in-my-body as you begin to notice the baby move. Some moms-to-be like to talk to their baby or pat their belly. Such actions are far from silly—they're the beginnings of bonding.

SECOND TRIMESTER CHECKLIST

✓ Schedule and have your checkups. (See pages 27–29.)

☐ Find a childbirth class. (See pages 30–31.)

✓ Tour the hospital or birthing center. *virtually*

✓ Preregister at the hospital or center if required.

☐ Choose a birth assistant, if you wish. (See pages 32–33.)

☐ Get recommendations for pediatricians.

☐ Fix things around the house that need it.

☐ Study the pros and cons of circumcision.

☐ Start planning for the nursery.

☐ Take photos and collect keepsakes.

Breast pump

CHECKING IN

Here's the place to take note of your feelings, observations, and milestones during the second trimester. Use this page also to take note of things to remember or to follow up. Or just doodle—relaxation is good for you.

SECOND TRIMESTER DOS AND DON'TS

DO . . .

- Enjoy the bloom and bursts of energy, as you experience them. Admire your changing shape in the mirror. Accept compliments gracefully.
- Continue taking prenatal vitamins.
- Be sure to consume enough protein.
- Use common sense when exercising. Stretch beforehand. Quit when you become over-exerted and don't allow yourself to become overheated.
- Take advantage of the "sexy surge" if it happens to you. Surging hormones often make women feel especially frisky in the middle months.
- Travel, if you can. Chances are that you feel good and, if you get a positive bill of health, can enjoy time alone or with your partner in a fairly unencumbered way.
- Wear a seatbelt in the car every time.
- Enjoy your partner. Go to a movie, throw a (low-key) party, dine out, plan a babymoon.

DON'T . . .

- Eat for two. Nope, still not true.
- Believe everything you hear. There's nothing like a visibly pregnant woman to invite advice, comments, and strange-but-supposedly true tales of how to determine an unborn baby's gender, health, or personality.
- Expect to feel like anybody else. Comparing notes with other pregnant women can be helpful, but only to a point.
- Leave your primary health care provider out of the loop. If you become interested in an alternative therapy, whether it's a botanical product, hypnosis, acupuncture, sound therapy, or something else, consult your doctor or midwife. Be aware that some alternative therapies are unstudied in pregnancy.
- Overdo it. Take breaks more often than you used to, too, and make sure you get at least seven to eight hours sleep at night.
- Skip obstetric visits if you feel fine. It's important for the health of you and your baby to be monitored at the regular intervals recommended by your doctor or midwife. (Record the details on the pages that follow.)

SECOND TRIMESTER CHECKUPS

Continue prenatal checkups as directed by your health care practitioner. During the second trimester you'll likely be visiting your practitioner at least once every four weeks. Take note of details. Keep your questions and concerns, and the responses to them, handy.

Date/time .... Practitioner ....

Weight.............................. Blood pressure .... Pulse ....

Fundus height .... Fetal heart rate ....

My questions & concerns ....

....

....

Responses & instructions ....

....

....

TESTS DONE OR ORDERED ....

....

Details and results ....

....

Follow up ....

Date/time .... Practitioner ....

Weight .... Blood pressure .... Pulse ....

Fundus height .... Fetal heart rate ....

My questions & concerns ....

....

....

Responses & instructions ....

....

....

TESTS DONE OR ORDERED ....

....

Details and results ....

....

Follow up ....

Notes ....

....

....

....

Date/time .... Practitioner ....

Weight .... Blood pressure .... Pulse ....

Fundus height .... Fetal heart rate ....

My questions & concerns ....

....

....

Responses & instructions ....

....

....

TESTS DONE OR ORDERED ....

....

Details and results ....

....

Follow up ....

Notes ....

....

....

CHOOSING A CHILDBIRTH CLASS

Read up on the various types of childbirth classes—from Bradley and Lamaze to ICEA—to decide which one resonates with you. Then use these questions to zero in on a particular class.

	CLASS 1
NAME OF CLASS	
Location	
Contact name and phone/email	
Where and when are classes?	
How long do they last (one long day; once a week for six weeks)? Will they be finished more than three weeks before my due date?	
What is the philosophy guiding the classes (especially for pain management or relaxation)?	
What do the classes cover (vaginal and cesarean birth, drug-free and drug-assisted labor, recovery, newborn care)?	
What is the instructor's certification and training?	
Is the instructor available by phone or e-mail?	
What do I need to provide? Do I need to bring someone?	
What is the fee?	
How many people are enrolled?	
Can I preview a class?	

CLASS 2	CLASS 3

CHOOSING A BIRTH ASSISTANT

Some parents decide to hire a birthing partner, or assistant, commonly called a doula, to make sure all bases are covered.

	BIRTH ASSISTANT 1
NAME OF BIRTH ASSISTANT	
Contact information	
Date and time of interview	
Where do you help deliver babies?	
How far do you live or work from my chosen site?	
How would you help in case of emergency cesarean?	
How many births have you assisted?	
How many high-risk pregnancies have you handled?	
What is your experience with my birthing place and my health practitioner, if any?	
Are you on call the two weeks before and after my due date?	
Who sees me if you are not available?	
What do you think about pain management?	
What specific support can you provide during labor?	
Details of costs and coverage	
What is your training? How long have you been practicing?	
To which professional groups do you belong?	
What classes do you recommend and when?	
Notes	

BIRTH ASSISTANT 2	BIRTH ASSISTANT 3

GETTING READY FOR BABY

Preparing for the baby is a unimester that overlaps all three trimesters. The main part of preparation is emotional, as parents-to-be get used to thinking of themselves and their world in a whole new way. Relationships will change and undergo stress, so it will be important to be flexible and patient. If there is a sibling, make sure they know the baby "belongs" to them as well and that they know what to expect. Siblings will need extra attention. Similarly, pets need to be prepared, too. Introduce them to the nursery and the new little interloper, making sure you continue to give them attention and space.

And then there are the practical preparations, from lining up the pediatrician to preparing the nursery, and from stocking up on baby supplies to scrutinizing child care options.

BABY PREP CHECKLIST

Research and choose a doctor for your child. (See pages 36–37.)

Think about names that you like. (See page 40.)

Research and line up child care, as needed.

Shop for needed baby equipment and supplies. (See pages 38–39.)

Stock your kitchen with basics needed for "easy meals."

Collect basic baby clothing.

Prepare the nursery.

Keep up with sleep and a healthful diet.

Clear away clutter and get paperwork in order.

Read about breast-feeding and infant formulas.

Take photos and collect keepsakes.

CHECKING IN

Here's the place to take note of your feelings, observations, and milestones as you prepare for baby. Use this page also to take note of things to remember or to follow up. Or just doodle—relaxation is good for you.

CHOOSING A PEDIATRICIAN

A good pediatrician often has a waiting list. Starting the search now makes sense.

	PEDIATRICIAN 1
NAME OF PEDIATRICIAN	
Contact information	
Date and time of interview	
What are the office hours, length of visits, and average wait?	
Can I speak with a doctor over the phone? Will there be charges for that?	
How do you handle non-urgent and after-hours questions? Email? Communicate through nurse?	
Who sees me when the doctor is not available?	
What tests do you do and when?	
Which procedures do nurses and assistants perform?	
What does the office do about sick children who are waiting?	
Details of costs and coverage	
What is your training? How long have you been practicing?	
Are you board certified in pediatrics? Do you have your own children?	
Do you have strong feelings about any of the following? Alternative medicine Breast-feeding Bottle feeding Circumcision Immunizations Teaching the baby to sleep Toilet training	
Notes (friendliness of staff, comfort in conversations)	

Note: The office staff may be able to answer many of the questions by phone.

PEDIATRICIAN 2	PEDIATRICIAN 3

BABY EQUIPMENT AND SUPPLIES CHECKLIST

It can be fun to collect needed items over time, as you run errands or find friends who are willing to lend larger items.

SLEEPING

- [ ] Crib
- [ ] Blankets
- [ ] Fitted crib sheets
- [ ] Waterproof mattress cover
- [ ] Baby monitor
- [ ] Humidifier or vaporizer
- [ ] Music player
- [ ] Mobile for crib

CHANGING

- [ ] Changing table
- [ ] Changing pad & cover
- [ ] Disposable diapers
- [ ] Cloth diapers & covers
- [ ] Diaper pail
- [ ] Baby wipes
- [ ] Powder with no talc

BATHING

- [ ] Infant tub
- [ ] Baby clippers and nail file
- [ ] Baby comb and brush
- [ ] Baby shampoo & soap
- [ ] Hooded towels
- [ ] Washcloths

FEEDING *(Note: Whether you breast-feed, bottle feed, or both affects the choices.)*

- [ ] Nursing bras & pads
- [ ] Support pillow
- [ ] Breast pump
- [ ] Bottles with collars, caps, & nipples
- [ ] Bottle brush
- [ ] Formula
- [ ] Sterilizer
- [ ] Bibs
- [ ] Burping cloths

DRESSING

- [ ] Booties
- [ ] Bottoms
- [ ] T-shirts
- [ ] Cotton or light cap
- [ ] Onesies (short and long sleeves)
- [ ] Pajamas
- [ ] Sleep sack
- [ ] Socks
- [ ] Special events outfit
- [ ] Sun hat
- [ ] Sweater or sweatshirt that opens in front
- [ ] Winter coat & hat if cold

GETTING AROUND

- [ ] Baby carrier
- [ ] Stroller
- [ ] Stroller cover
- [ ] Stroller toys
- [ ] Infant car seat
- [ ] Car blanket
- [ ] Shades for car windows
- [ ] Toys to hang in car
- [ ] Diaper bag
- [ ] Insulated bottle carrier
- [ ] Overnight bag
- [ ] Portable changing pad
- [ ] Portable sleeping crib
  - [ ] Fitted sheets
  - [ ] Mattress
  - [ ] Traveling blankets
  - [ ] Waterproof mattress cover

BABY SUPPLIES

- [ ] Medical book
- [ ] Thermometer
- [ ] Baby acetaminophen
- [ ] Lotion
- [ ] Antibiotic cream
- [ ] Hydrogen peroxide
- [ ] Petroleum jelly
- [ ] Rubbing alcohol
- [ ] Bandages
- [ ] Cotton balls
- [ ] Ipecac syrup
- [ ] Medicine dropper, spoon, syringe
- [ ] Nasal aspirator
- [ ] Pacifiers
- [ ] Tweezers

PLAYING

- [ ] Basket for toys
- [ ] Bouncy seat
- [ ] Music
- [ ] Play links
- [ ] Play mat
- [ ] Rattles
- [ ] Soft blocks
- [ ] Soft books
- [ ] Swing

OTHER

- [ ] Dresser
- [ ] Rocking chair or glider
- [ ] Night light
- [ ] Hamper
- [ ] Shelves & bins
- [ ] Outlet covers
- [ ] Books about breast-feeding, child care, parenting
- [ ] Baby book and journal

NAMES

Naming the baby is fun. You may choose a name, only to change your mind upon meeting your son or daughter. But here are some tips to help you through the process.

- Look at baby-naming websites or books for ideas.
- List names you know and like the sound of.
- Write names down. Say them aloud.
- Consider the full name, including the middle name, and the initials.
- Think about the options that attract you. Do you like traditional names? Original names?
- Do you like names that could be given to either a boy or a girl?
- What are the nicknames that people might make?
- Are there family names you want to include?

List your top contenders here.

GIRL NAMES	BOY NAMES

THIRD TRIMESTER

The last trimester of pregnancy is an especially exciting time of your life because You Are Definitely About to Have a Baby! You look it, and feel it. Strangers can tell. The more frequent doctor visits say so, too.

Take advantage of these weeks to make final plans and preparations for motherhood. With your partner, compare notes about your feelings during these countdown weeks and share expectations about baby care and finding time for your relationship after you become parents.

And leave time to dream a little, too. The last three months of pregnancy are a time for wondering, waiting, wishing, and—yes— waiting.

THIRD TRIMESTER CHECKLIST

Schedule and have your checkups. (See pages 44–52.)

Take childbirth classes. (See page 53.)

Start tracking fetal movements. (See pages 54–56.)

Write up a birth plan. (See pages 57–60.)

Ready birth announcement list.

Learn about newborn and baby care.

Look for other new moms for support.

Finalize work plans and maternity leave.

Finalize child care, if needed.

Finish stocking and decorating nursery.

Pack the labor bag and diaper bag. (See pages 61–62.)

Install infant seat in car.

Stock the kitchen.

Take photos and collect keepsakes.

CHECKING IN

Here's the place to take note of your feelings, observations, and milestones during the third trimester. Use this page also to take note of things to remember or to follow up. Or just doodle—relaxation is good for you.

THIRD TRIMESTER DOS AND DON'TS

DO . . .

- Expect to gain about 1 to 1-1/2 pounds a week this trimester.
- Eat lots of small meals to accommodate your stomach being compressed.
- Drink lots of water. Staying well-hydrated enhances blood production, wards off constipation, and may help you avoid premature contractions.
- Continue taking your prenatal vitamins.
- Take care to stand tall and grounded.
- Keep moving. Exercise makes you feel better and helps your body to prepare for delivery.
- Rehearse your delivery. Know how to reach your partner at all times by the ninth month and have a backup plan for getting to the hospital.
- Take care of hospital or birthing center admittance paperwork ahead of time.
- Do kick counts to monitor your baby's well-being.
- Read up on breast-feeding and parenting techniques while you have the time.
- Use your journal to write about your worries as well as your wishes.

DON'T . . .

- Be too impatient. The weeks may seem to tick by slowly, but you should take advantage of this time to prepare yourself mentally and practically for parenthood.
- Skip the seat belt because it's uncomfortable. You're buckling up for two.
- Overdo it. Listen to your body, which may be signaling a need for increased rest as your pregnancy progresses. Aim for a balance between moving and relaxing.
- Use stepstools or ladders, or otherwise put yourself at risk for falls.
- Ignore bothersome symptoms or hesitate to call and ask your doctor about anything.
- Pretend you're not pregnant. It may sound hard to ignore the physical reality, but many women also try to deny the mental reality by avoiding talking about or thinking about the baby growing inside them.

THIRD TRIMESTER CHECKUPS

Continue prenatal checkups as directed by your health care practitioner. During the third trimester you'll likely be visiting your practitioner bi-weekly from week 28 to week 34, and weekly from the 36th week onward. Take note of details. Keep your questions and concerns, and the responses to them, handy.

Date/time .... Practitioner ....

Weight...................................... Blood pressure .... Pulse ....

Fundus height .... Fetal heart rate ....

My questions & concerns ....

....

....

Responses & instructions ....

....

....

TESTS DONE OR ORDERED ....

....

Details and results ....

....

Follow up ....

Date/time .... Practitioner ....

Weight .... Blood pressure ....Pulse ....

Fundus height .... Fetal heart rate ....

My questions & concerns ....

....

....

Responses & instructions ....

....

....

TESTS DONE OR ORDERED ....

....

Details and results ....

....

Follow up ....

Notes ....

....

....

....

Date/time .... Practitioner ....

Weight .... Blood pressure ....Pulse ....

Fundus height .... Fetal heart rate ....

My questions & concerns ....

....

....

Responses & instructions ....

....

....

TESTS DONE OR ORDERED ....

....

Details and results ....

....

Follow up ....

Notes ....

....

....

....

Date/time .... Practitioner ....

Weight .... Blood pressure .... Pulse ....

Fundus height .... Fetal heart rate ....

My questions & concerns ....

....

....

Responses & instructions ....

....

....

TESTS DONE OR ORDERED ....

....

Details and results ....

....

Follow up ....

Notes ....

....

....

....

Date/time .... Practitioner ....

Weight .... Blood pressure .... Pulse ....

Fundus height .... Fetal heart rate ....

My questions & concerns ....

....

....

Responses & instructions ....

....

....

TESTS DONE OR ORDERED ....

....

Details and results ....

....

Follow up ....

Notes ....

....

....

Date/time .... Practitioner ....

Weight .... Blood pressure .... Pulse ....

Fundus height .... Fetal heart rate ....

My questions & concerns ....

....

....

Responses & instructions ....

....

....

TESTS DONE OR ORDERED ....

....

Details and results ....

....

Follow up ....

Notes ....

....

....

Date/time .... Practitioner ....

Weight .... Blood pressure ....Pulse ....

Fundus height .... Fetal heart rate ....

My questions & concerns ....

....

....

Responses & instructions ....

....

....

TESTS DONE OR ORDERED ....

....

Details and results ....

....

Follow up ....

Notes ....

....

....

....

Date/time .... Practitioner ....

Weight .... Blood pressure .... Pulse ....

Fundus height .... Fetal heart rate ....

My questions & concerns ....

....

....

Responses & instructions ....

....

....

TESTS DONE OR ORDERED ....

....

Details and results ....

....

Follow up ....

Notes ....

....

....

....

Date/time .... Practitioner ....

Weight .... Blood pressure .... Pulse ....

Fundus height .... Fetal heart rate ....

My questions & concerns ....

....

....

Responses & instructions ....

....

....

TESTS DONE OR ORDERED ....

....

Details and results ....

....

Follow up ....

Notes ....

....

....

....

CHILDBIRTH CLASS NOTES

If you haven't chosen a childbirth class yet, refer back to pages 30-31 for guidance. Find a class that ends at least three weeks before your due date. This page helps you keep track of classmates, along with questions and answers.

Name and location of class: ....

....

Teacher's name: ....

Questions to ask in class: ....

....

....

....

Responses: ....

....

....

....

Contact info for other parents (or parents-to-be): ....

....

....

....

....

FETAL MOVEMENT CHARTS

Feeling your baby move is not only precious, it's also a helpful way to monitor his or her health. The medical community recommends that, around 28 weeks, you begin paying special attention to the frequency of movements.

Choose a time when your baby frequently seems most active, then record how long it takes to feel 10 movements. If you notice a significant deviation from the baby's movement pattern over the course of a few days or if you haven't felt 10 movements in two hours (first have a snack or a glass of juice and try again), contact your doctor or midwife.

	SU	M	TU	W	TH	F	SA
WEEK 28							
Start							
End							
Time it takes to reach 10							
WEEK 29							
Start							
End							
Time it takes to reach 10							
WEEK 30							
Start							
End							
Time it takes to reach 10							

	SU	M	TU	W	TH	F	SA
WEEK 31							
Start							
End							
Time it takes to reach 10							
WEEK 32							
Start							
End							
Time it takes to reach 10							
WEEK 33							
Start							
End							
Time it takes to reach 10							
WEEK 34							
Start							
End							
Time it takes to reach 10							
WEEK 35							
Start							
End							
Time it takes to reach 10							

	SU	M	TU	W	TH	F	SA

WEEK 36

Start							
End							
Time it takes to reach 10							

WEEK 37

Start							
End							
Time it takes to reach 10							

WEEK 38

Start							
End							
Time it takes to reach 10							

WEEK 39

Start							
End							
Time it takes to reach 10							

WEEK 40

Start							
End							
Time it takes to reach 10							

THE BIRTH PLAN

At the last minute, you don't want to have to explain yourself. Set up a birth plan in advance, but keep in mind that not all labor and deliveries go as planned. You cannot control every detail of the birth, but you can make your preferences known. To do so, learn about and thoughtfully consider childbirth procedure options—from fetal monitoring to episiotomy—and with guidance from your doctor or midwife, create your wish list. Some women provide one-page copies of their plans to the hospital or birthing center, the medical practitioner, and the labor coach.

Here is what you need to ask yourself in order to consider options:

What is your first choice location for the birth? (Hospital? Birth center? Home?)

Whom do you want with you?

What are your lighting or music preferences?

Video or photography requests?

What would you hope for regarding food and drink during early labor? ....

....

....

What is your preference about constant external fetal monitoring for baby? ....

....

Internal fetal monitoring? ....

....

What methods do you prefer for comfort and pain relief? ....

....

....

....

At what point would pain medication be welcome? How will you say so? ....

....

....

Which birthing method is preferred? ....

....

Who would you like present in the case of a Cesarean delivery? ....

....

Would you like to move around or bathe or shower during labor? ....

....

....

Would you like to squat? Recline? Have people or pedals for support? ....

....

....

What do you hope for with regard to having an episiotomy? ....

....

Would you like to view the birth in a mirror? ....

....

What are your thoughts about the following:

    • Inducing labor? ....

    • IV? ....

    • Forceps and/or vacuum extraction? ....

Who cuts the cord and when (after it stop pulsing or immediately)? ....

....

Will the cord blood be banked? Have you made arrangements? ....

....

How do you feel about IV medication, including pitocin? ....

....

How do you picture first holding and feeding the baby? ....

....

....

Where will the baby first sleep? Who will care for the baby?...

....

....

Who gets to visit? ....

....

....

Breast-feeding or bottle or both? Pacifier? ....

....

If you have a boy, do you want him to be circumcised? ....

Other wishes? ....

....

....

....

....

LABOR BAG CHECKLISTS

Eighty percent of women have babies within two weeks before or after their due dates. So why not pack for the hospital a month in advance? Before packing, find out whether cell phones are allowed and where.

MOM'S BAG

- [ ] Hospital or birth center preregistration
- [ ] Health insurance card
- [ ] Copies of birth plan
- [ ] List of contacts to call with news
- [ ] Journal
- [ ] Reading material
- [ ] Toiletries, including lip balm, maxipads
- [ ] Eyeglasses
- [ ] Something to clip or hold hair
- [ ] Comfy socks
- [ ] Robe
- [ ] Slippers
- [ ] Nightgown that can be ruined (if preferred to hospital gown)
- [ ] Nightgown for breast-feeding
- [ ] Half dozen pairs of panties
- [ ] Two bras
- [ ] Comfortable stretchy outfit to wear home
- [ ] Object to focus on during labor
- [ ] Cell phone and charger, if allowed

PARTNER'S BAG

- [ ] Phone numbers
- [ ] Cell phone and charger, if allowed
- [ ] Snacks and beverages
- [ ] Extra cash, including change for vending machines
- [ ] Reading material
- [ ] Playing cards
- [ ] Paper and writing utensil
- [ ] Labor and breast-feeding handbooks or sheets
- [ ] Massage tools
- [ ] Portable music player, if needed
- [ ] Watch or clock with second hand
- [ ] Toiletries
- [ ] Bathing suit if showering
- [ ] Change of clothes

BABY'S DIAPER BAG

For first trip home:

- [ ] Baby mittens to cover nails
- [ ] Booties or socks
- [ ] Cotton or knit cap
- [ ] Blanket
- [ ] Newborn outfit
- [ ] Burping cloths

For always:

- [ ] Antibacterial hand cleaner
- [ ] Baby wipes
- [ ] Card with emergency numbers
- [ ] Changing pad
- [ ] Clean baby outfit
- [ ] Diapers
- [ ] Formula and bottle
- [ ] Lotion for diaper rash
- [ ] Plastic bags for dirties
- [ ] Small first aid kit
- [ ] Sun or cold-weather hat as needed
- [ ] Water

Extras:

- [ ] Pacifier
- [ ] Shirt for Mom
- [ ] Snack for Mom
- [ ] Toy(s)

BAG FOR BROTHERS AND SISTERS

- [ ] Snacks
- [ ] Paper and drawing utensils
- [ ] Reading materials
- [ ] Toys
- [ ] Secret gifts for Mom, baby, and/ or siblings

CONTRACTION CHART

Early labor can last a long time, even eight or more hours. You will begin to feel contractions at regular intervals, about 10 to 20 minutes apart and lasting about 30 seconds. Gradually contractions become closer together, to about 5 to 7 minutes apart, and longer, to about 40 to 60 seconds long.

Provided your water hasn't broken and unless you have medical advice to the contrary, it's generally a good idea to spend early labor in the comfort of your own home. Use the chart below to keep track of your contractions. Keep in mind the correct way to measure time between contractions is to note the starting time of one contraction and count how many minutes pass until the start of the next.

TIME OF START	TIME OF END	DURATION	TIME BETWEEN CONTRACTIONS

LIST FOR LABOR PARTNER

At the hospital or birthing center, make sure the mom and the staff understand one another. Note that cell phones are not allowed in some maternity wards, as the signals can interfere with some equipment. Ask before dialing.

Is it time? Ready . . . set . . . go! The list below will help the labor partner stay focused during this exciting time.

NEED TO TRANSPORT

- Infant seat
- Bag for mom
- Your bag
- Baby's bag
- Bag for siblings
- Master list of phone numbers (i.e. this book)
- Mom's medical records

DURING EARLY LABOR

- Time contractions.
- Call doctor or midwife.
- Call the people needed for the birth (doula, family, friends).
- Call anyone helping with children or pets.
- Call work.

ARRIVAL AT PLACE OF BIRTH

- Take care of paperwork.
- Request private room for recovery if desired.

DURING LABOR AND DELIVERY

- Do what is possible to help Mom.
- Communicate her needs with the staff.

AFTER BIRTH

You can help to:

- Square away pain management concerns.
- Check on the baby's care.
- Inform the pediatrician.
- Arrange for lactation specialist, if desired.
- Arrange for birth certificate.
- Arrange for prints of the baby's hands and feet.
- Make birth announcements.
- Keep track of flowers and gifts received at hospital.
- Get a breast pump, if needed.
- Take photos and videos.

LEAVING FOR HOME

- Pack the bags.
- Collect the paperwork in one place.
- Arrange for transportation home.

MASTER LIST OF PHONE NUMBERS

You may forget your own name, much less those of people who need to know. When making this list, think of things that could go wrong. Line up alternates for sitters and drivers. You just never know!

Hospital or center ....

Insurance company ....

Obstetrician ....

Midwife ....

Birth assistant ....

Sitter for siblings ....

Sitter for pets ....

Pediatrician ....

Pharmacy ....

Lactation consultant ....

Family, friends, neighbors ....

....

....

Vet/Kennel ....

Taxi ....

Other ....

BIRTH AND BEYOND

Congratulations—you've done it! Take time to appreciate the miracle that is your brand-new baby. Remember that loving your little child is more important than all the to-do lists in the world. On the other hand—like most new mothers—you will resolve to do everything necessary to make sure your baby is well cared for.

Your body has done something truly amazing and wonderful in creating a new life. Celebrate that singular fact! Feel proud of yourself and your accomplishment, whether or not labor unfolded exactly the way you'd hoped and wished.

Parents change the baby, but the baby changes everything for the parents. Your old routines have flown out the window. As you adjust to your new normal, many issues—from breast-feeding (or not) to birth control to regaining your figure to fitting your old life and your new life together—need to be addressed.

After all the highs and lows you have been through, postpartum depression (PPD) or some form of "baby blues" is pretty common, due to hormonal changes and dramatic life change. If depression or anxiety strikes, tell your partner, your friends, and your doctor. Get help with tasks, and take care of yourself with good sleeping, eating, and exercise habits.

This is a good time to be as compassionate and nonjudgmental with yourself and your partner as you are with your new baby. It's also a good time to refrain from over-analyzing your life, at least for several months. Embrace the chaos while keeping plans simple and fluid.

Other new parents offer the insight that rather than striving to be perfect it's better to cultivate your *own* parenting style and your *own* way of integrating competing needs of family members, work, and household. And make sure to fit your own needs into the equation.

Now that you're a parent, with all the attendant concerns, allow yourself the full measure of joy as well.

BIRTH AND BEYOND CHECKLIST

- [ ] Keep track of baby's sleeping, feeding, and diapering details
- [ ] Journal feelings and firsts.
- [ ] Schedule your postnatal appointment. (See page 70.)
- [ ] Schedule baby's first checkup. (See page 71.)
- [ ] Get print of baby's hands and feet.
- [ ] Ask for itemized bill and copies of paperwork.
- [ ] Get Social Security card (U.S.) or register baby (U.K.).
- [ ] Tell insurance company.
- [ ] Take photos and collect keepsakes.
- [ ] Send out announcements.
- [ ] Get a birth certificate.
- [ ] Line up help, if needed (household, lactation, respite care, grocery delivery, etc).
- [ ] Play music to soothe the soul.
- [ ] Sign up for postpartum exercise class.
- [ ] Congratulate yourself!

MY CHILDBIRTH STORY

When all is said and done, you may still have more to say, so here are pages to fill with your memories. Add details about your newborn on page 72.

When we knew baby was on the way

Whom we called

What happened next

Biggest surprise during labor

Who was there

What labor was like

Baby's birth

What happened next ....

....

....

Who said what ....

....

What was amazing ....

....

....

In the hours that followed ....

....

....

In the days that followed...

....

....

Wishes and hopes for baby: ....

....

....

....

POSTNATAL APPOINTMENT

Keep track of questions for the ob/gyn, nurse, or midwife, along with results of the postnatal appointment, normally scheduled for six weeks after the birth.

Date/time .... Practitioner ....

Weight .... Blood pressure ....Pulse ....

Pap/pelvic ....

My questions & concerns (driving, excercise, sex and birth control, bathing) ....

....

....

Responses & instructions ....

....

....

TESTS DONE OR ORDERED ....

....

Details and results ....

....

Follow up ....

Next appointment ....

BABY'S FIRST DOCTOR VISIT

Your baby's first checkup will be scheduled within the first few weeks of birth. Be prepared to report on your baby's eating, sleeping, and overall progress. Bring in your questions, and take note of the doctor's responses and instructions.

Date and time .... Doctor's name ....

Baby's weight .... Baby's length ....Head circumference ....

Immunizations ....

My questions & concerns ....

....

....

....

Responses & instructions ....

....

....

TESTS DONE OR ORDERED ....

....

Details and results ....

....

Follow up ....

Next appointment ....

BABY NOTES

Baby's full name and nicknames..

The inspiration for the name ....

Due date... Actual date of birth ....

Time of birth .... Place of birth ....

Baby was delivered by ....

The people who helped included ....

Baby came out ▢ head first ▢ feet first ▢ via Caesarean

Weight .... Height .... Length ....

Circumference of head .... Circumference of chest ....

APGAR at 1 minute .... APGAR at 5 minutes ....

Blood type ....

Hair description ....

Eye color ....

Other notes ....

....

....

....